Psongs of my Heart!

Written by Bee Glasscho
Cover illustration by Cameron Glasscho

Copyright © 2022 All rights reserved. No part of this publication may be reproduced, distributed, or transmitted in any form or by any means, including photocopying, recording, or other electronic or mechanical methods, without the prior written permission of the publisher, except in the case of brief quotations embodied in critical reviews and certain other noncommercial uses permitted by copyright law.

Unless otherwise noted, scripture quotations in this book are from New International Version. Biblica, 2011. Bible Gateway,

www.biblegateway.com/versions/New- International-Version-NIV-Bible/ Wright, N.T., translator.

The Kingdom New Testament: A Contemporary Translation

Book Design by HMDpublishing

Acknowledgements

First and most importantly, I want to thank my Lord and Savior Jesus Christ who gave his life in exchange for mine. He has given us all an opportunity to be saved, healed and restored in Him. All glory to God for allowing this journey to come into fruition. My love and gratitude are inexplicable and I'm eternally grateful for the gifts He has given me. I'd also like to thank my mom, Burujah aka Omi, for birthing me into this world and giving me a foundation to build upon. Without my mama, there would be no me!! I love you to the moon and beyond mommy.

Also, the publishing of this book could not have been completed without the love, support and encouragement of my beautiful girls Nafeesah, Sierra, Aniya, and Jaida—you've all inspired me to want better and to do better, especially when my life felt unlivable. Included in my growth and gratitude are my bonus children Justin and Cameron. Thank you both for accepting, supporting and loving me at my best and worst of times. You all are my greatest treasures and have captured my whole heart.

D. Rahn Glasscho, my husband, best friend, and the love of my life-- Thank you for supporting and believing in me. Your prayers and encouragement have helped to strengthen me during my doubts and uncertainties. You have opened parts of my heart that I never knew existed and I thank God for you! Our love is one of a kind and so are you!

Lastly, I want to thank my biological and also chosen sisters and brothers: Mecca S., Radiah S., Maryam A., my sousin Toni H., Jennifer B., Makita @ Peace R., Rachel R., Rica H., Nikki H., Monyelle "Nikki" D., Theresa B., Marlene M., Newton M., Tatina B., Robine B, Darrell B.; my cousins Regina W., Joanne W., Zina "Denise", Safiyya J., Ashley H., Vicki P., Loretta F.; my nieces and nephews Niesha F., Melina W., Aliyah B., Joy M. , Journey M., Nia B., Thierry W., Lovelle S.; my extended family, Archie "Trey"A. and Rakan D., Bishop Ruth, Apostle Frederick H.; and all of my aunties and uncles-- you all have loved, supported, encouraged and/or prayed for me during some very tough times of this journey, I truly love and thank you all!

Finally, I have a special shout out to the grandest blessings of this journey my G-baby Autumn Akeerah A. and GG-babies Nolan and Naudia W., and my great niece and nephew Jamari N. and Jelina J. May you be the next generation that serves and surrenders to the Lord. Hallelujah!

About the Author

Bee Glasscho is a writer, author, and poet, who had both a gift and calling in the arts which showed at an early age. She was born in Corona Queens, NY and raised as a Sunni Muslim in Newark, NJ by a single mother of three. Bee found herself having children out of wedlock and eventually gave her life to Christ. As a single mother, she completed her Bachelor's degree in science and went on to pursue a career in corporate America... Only to realize that it created depression and bondage that would force her to seek out God and find out her true purpose. After multiple failed relationships, poor life choices, and living a desolate existence as a middle-class single mom, she decided to chase after the True and Living God for answers and comfort. Eventually, she realized her search for an abundant life in Christ uncovered the depths of the pain that lived deep in her heart and tormented her soul since childhood. Poetry became a journaling outlet that eventually helped to heal, restore and redeem her through the word of God. She married an imperfect man who sought after God's heart and ultimately captured hers! By perfectly blending their two families and growing in their faith at the same time, they've managed to create a life of joy and peace that she had often dreamed about.

Contents

How It Started	7
Innocence	8
Salvation	10
Love	12
The Stranger	15
It's me!	17
The Blank Void	20
Breathe Again	22
Reflections	24
The Mirror	25
Hide and Seek	27
Forgiving	30
A smile	32
Can You See Me?	34
Get Ready!!!	38
Nothing	41
Betrayal	43
The Thief In the Night	44
Weapons	47
Unauthorized Touches	50
A woman scorned	53
Repentence	56
True Friend	59
Deceit	62
Relationships	65
Possible Potential	66
Toxic Friendships	69
The Rebound Chick	72

Love to be loved..75
Heart Guardian..78
New Dog-Old Tricks!...81
I See You! 84

Parenting..86

A Single Mother's Cry 87
Help Me!!! 89
Sweet Baby Girls 92
The Bigger Me!! 95
You are not my father..97
The LOVE poem 100
A Borrowed Blessing 102

Acknowledgment 105

This Experience...106
The Courage to love 109
And it works'...112
Why?...115
A Queen 117
Choices 119
Mistakes 122

Redemption...125

Healing...126
Count it All Joy!..129
Eviction Notice 132
His Will..135
Suds of Hope 138
The Battle is Won!!..141
The Cure...144

Bonus Poems 147

Free!..148
The Prophetic Warrior 151
God's Grace 154

How It Started

Innocence

She was so small and delicate, innocent and pure
As she lays in her bed there was a knock at her door
The knock was soft and the voice familiar
But the touch on her shoulder felt a little peculiar
Too afraid to speak she laid still as if she was sleep
But the boy didn't leave, he was playing for keeps
He touched her in places where he should not put his hands
She was too frail and afraid to take a courageous stand
She felt violated and shameful, her soul was hollow
Unable to speak or cry, nor could she swallow
She felt pain but didn't realize she'd been scarred for life
She had no idea that she harbored so much anger and strife
Innocence stolen in the blink of an eye
Leaving a little girl wondering "why me, why"?
She doesn't trust men, her innocence now gone
How can she LIVE when she wishes she was NEVER born

Proverbs 29:25- Fearing people is a dangerous trap, but trusting the LORD means safety.

Colossians 1:21-22- This includes you who were once far away from God. You were his enemies, separated from him by your evil thoughts and actions. ²² Yet now he has reconciled you to himself through the death of Christ in his physical body. As a result, he has brought you into his own presence, and you are holy and blameless as you stand before him without a single fault.

2 Chronicles 6:23- then hear from heaven and judge between your servants—the accuser and the accused. Pay back the guilty as they deserve. Acquit the innocent because of their **innocence**.

Hebrews 2:2 - For the message God delivered through angels has always stood firm, and every violation of the law and every act of disobedience was punished.

From My Journey to Yours

Salvation

A child badly beaten with a heart beating near dead
Always dreaming about Prince charming as she lay in her bed
Hoping for the day she is saved from the torment of herself
She realizes the day won't come until she calls on God for help
Her physical body growing, and on the outside, she has bloomed
On the inside her spirit broken from the abuse suffered in her bedroom
Beatings and molestation have fragmented her soul
Joy, peace, and happiness are lost in a deep dark hole
Her secrets are unbearable, her heart a heavy stone
Her feelings of true freedom come in the form of a bag of bones
As time begins to pass, her reality shows the truth
That the beginning of her salvation really started in her youth.

1 Timothy 4:12- Don't let anyone think less of you because you are young. Be an example to all believers in what you say, in the way you live, in your love, your faith, and your purity.

Psalm 62:2 -He alone is my rock and my salvation, my fortress where I will never be shaken.

Isaiah 30:20 - Though the Lord gave you adversity for food and suffering for drink, he will still be with you to teach you. You will see your teacher with your own eyes.

Psalm 51:12 - Restore to me the joy of your salvation, and make me willing to obey you.

From My Journey to Yours

Love

I hate you, I hate you—That's right, I spit in your face
You're dumb, you're nothing, you're meaningless--
Such a freak'in waste
You're ugly and you're stupid
I wish you were never born
Why are you still here? I wish you were gone.
You'll be pregnant by thirteen and won't amount to anything
You won't graduate high school –you're just a stupid fool
And you think you're better than me—?
I'll beat you black and blue and out of your eyes you won't see.
I'll burn you and beat you until you bow down to me
I'll cuss you and dog as much as I can, I'll bruise your soul and your pride
So, you can feel vulnerable at all times
I'll never protect you…but you'll learn how to survive
And you'll do things in life that surrenders your pride.
Your smile will be empty and your heart forever scorned
I'll sell your soul to the devil by soliciting it for porn
You're sitting on a million dollars and you don't have to beg
And the best part of you ran down your daddy's leg
With all that said sweet little girl, I love you so much
Here, come give me hug and let me feel your warm touch.

Psalm 69:20 -Their insults have broken my heart, and I am in despair. If only one person would show some pity; if only one would turn and comfort me.

Matthew 18:6 - But if you cause one of these little ones who trusts in me to fall into sin, it would be better for you to have a large millstone tied around your neck and be drowned in the depths of the sea.

1 Corinthians 13:4-7 Love is patient and kind. Love is not jealous or boastful or proud [5] or rude. It does not demand its own way. It is not irritable, and it keeps no record of being wronged. [6] It does not rejoice about injustice but rejoices whenever the truth wins out. ⁷Love never gives up, never loses faith, is always hopeful, and endures through every circumstance.

1 John 4:7-8 - Dear friends, let us continue to love one another, for love comes from God. Anyone who loves is a child of God and knows God. 8 But anyone who does not love does not know God, for God is love.

From My Journey to Yours

The Stranger

One morning I woke up and saw a stranger in my house
She didn't move or talk, she stayed as quiet as a mouse
Her eyes were almond shaped and were beautiful at first sight
But as I looked a little closer, I could see she'd been in a fight
Her hair was mangled and her face badly bruised
Her clothes were torn and she didn't have on shoes
Her outer appearance was badly battered and beaten
She also looked hungry as if it had been a while since she'd last eaten.
My heart was pounding, ferociously with fear
I was wondering "how in the world did she get in here"?
My alarm wasn't disabled and my bedroom door was still locked.
Her presence in my home was a mysterious shock
As I attempted to speak and extend my hand to help
She backed away from me with a loud piercing whelp
My heart became heavy as my eyes started to see
The stranger in my house was actually a reflection of me.

James 1:23-25 - For if you listen to the word and don't obey, it is like glancing at your face in a mirror. 24 You see yourself, walk away, and forget what you look like. 25 But if you look carefully into the perfect law that sets you free, and if you do what it says and don't forget what you heard, then God will bless you for doing it.

Isaiah 41:10 - Don't be afraid, for I am with you. Don't be discouraged, for I am your God.

I will strengthen you and help you. I will hold you up with my victorious right hand.

Psalm 91: 5-6 - Do not be afraid of the terrors of the night, nor the arrow that flies in the day.

6. Do not dread the disease that stalks in darkness, nor the disaster that strikes at midday.

From My Journey to Yours

It's me!

I gotta make a dollar out of fifteen cents
If I can't put my heart in it, it makes no sense
To say I'm ready to truly give my life to God
When I'm in the street to survive –that's why I struggle so hard
I'm not a man or woman who lies to the Almighty One
Right now, my only source of protection seems to be an almighty gun
I hold true to who I am, but I'm JUST human
Thinking I got the answers but no one understands
I don't have a way out and I'm stuck
Because I've been selling my soul to the almighty buck
I sit alone and I pray for the guidance I need
To prepare for liberation from the crooks and the thieves
This way of life is not easy to change in one day
And leaving it for good is something that I pray
Can happen in time as I seek the truth
Asking God to be delivered from the curses of my youth
I'm now a person enslaved by the shackles of my worldly master
But I'm running for my freedom-faster and faster
Survival is not peaceful-I'm imprisoned in my mind
Compassion and love in these streets-- I'll never find
That's why I pray in silence to be truly freed from this world
Can you hear my prayers Lord? I'm still your little girl
Yes, It's really me!

Romans 6:6 - We know that our old sinful selves were crucified with Christ so that sin might lose its power in our lives. We are no longer slaves to sin.

Luke 4:18 - "The Spirit of the Lord is upon me, for he has anointed me to bring Good News to the poor. He has sent me to proclaim that captives will be released, that the blind will see, that the oppressed will be set free,

Galatians 5:1- It is for freedom that Christ has set us free. Stand firm, then, and do not let yourselves be burdened again by a yoke of slavery.

Psalms 34:17- The righteous cry out, and the Lord hears them; he delivers them from all their troubles.

Psalms 50:15- and call on me in the day of trouble; I will deliver you, and you will honor me."

From My Journey to Yours

_____

_____

_____

_____

_____

_____

_____

_____

_____

_____

_____

The Blank Void
(inspired by Mecca Stinnette)

I don't know,I don't know-- I'm longing for the answers
I'm plagued with a death sentence, like being riddled by cancer
My own body is foreign to me because I never knew
While my physical body matured that my spirit NEVER grew
As I search for the abundance of peace and prosperity, it's hard for me to focus
There's nothing magical about healing this pain—I don't believe in hocus pocus!
Into a sea of darkness surrounded by bitterness and hatred—
I sit in the circle of fear and pain as if I'm really complacent
My identity, stolen and tossed aside as if it never existed
But I no longer want to forget because my realities are confused and twisted.
There's something I know exists but it's hard for me to find
The answers are here, but pushed to the back of my mind
I'm soaring high above the skies, moving as fast as an asteroid
Forever living in a sea of forgetfulness where I find my blank void

John 3:21-But whoever lives by the truth comes into the light, so that it may be seen plainly that what they have done has been done in the sight of God.

1 John 1:6- If we claim to have fellowship with him and yet walk in the darkness, we lie and do not live out the truth.

1 Corinthians 14:33- For God is not a God of disorder but of peace—as in all the congregations of the Lord's people.

Luke 8:17- For there is nothing hidden that will not be disclosed, and nothing concealed that will not be known or brought out into the open.

From My Journey to Yours

_____

_____

_____

_____

_____

_____

_____

_____

_____

_____

_____

_____

Breathe Again

I suddenly woke up and it was hard for me to breathe
It felt like something was obstructing my throat and causing me to wheeze
Then I started to think--what could make me to lose my breath?
My heart started pounding and I realized it was death
I've been dying in spirit from living for the world
Digging up rocks and gravel instead of God's beautiful pearls
I felt a deep dark heaviness hovering over my bed
In just a matter of seconds, I could be lying here dead
I called out the name of Jesus, and then my spirit opened up
I kept crying out of my soul, hearing the echo of my silent cup
And the echo's seemed further away as I called out His name
Jesus! Jesus! Jesus! There He was...He ACTUALLY came!
My chest still felt heavy as I felt my last breath
He quickly saved me from what felt like sudden death
Then the darkness and heavy feeling miraculously left
The darkness that surrounded me gave way to the light
God had shown me the Glory from His power and his might
While Satan thought he had me, the power of God ALWAYS wins
Cause in the name of Jesus I could breathe again!!

Romans 10:13- for, "Everyone who calls on the name of the Lord will be saved."

James 1:3-because you know that the testing of your faith produces perseverance.

James 4:7-Submit yourselves, then, to God. Resist the devil, and he will flee from you.

Ephesians 2:10- For we are God's handiwork, created in Christ Jesus to do good works, which God prepared in advance for us to do.

From My Journey to Yours

Reflections

The Mirror

When I look into the mirror, what do I see?
A distorted image of a woman staring right back at me
Her eyes are dark and desolate, her skin scarred and pale
Her hair is broken and damaged, and her smile is weak and frail
In her reflection is sadness far beyond compare
All of her heartaches and cries, no one could ever hear
But one day she heard someone ask her what was wrong
It was a voice she'd longed to hear from for 25 years long
Too afraid to answer and too ashamed to feel
She retreats back to silence, but wants to pray and kneel
As she looks back into the mirror her reflection isn't alone
She sees a glow behind her asking her to come home
In her heart she nods happily and truly wants to submit
But the image in the mirror thinks she is still unfit
To no avail the woman struggles and tries to find her way
Today she sees the sunshine of a brand-new brighter day
Will her image in the mirror set her free or make her stay?

Genesis 4:7-You will be accepted if you do what is right. But if you refuse to do what is right, then watch out! Sin is crouching at the door, eager to control you. But you must subdue it and be its master."

1 Corinthians: 11-12 - When I was a child, I spoke and thought and reasoned as a child. But when I grew up, I put away childish things. 12. Now we see things imperfectly, like puzzling reflections in a mirror, but then we will see everything with perfect clarity. All that I know now is partial and incomplete, but then I will know everything completely, just as God now knows me completely.

Romans 7:25- Thank God! The answer is in Jesus Christ our Lord. So you see how it is: In my mind I really want to obey God's law, but because of my sinful nature I am a slave to sin.

1 John 1:5 - This is the message we heard from Jesus[a] and now declare to you: God is light, and there is no darkness in him at all.

From My Journey to Yours

Hide and Seek

Inside that secret place that hides me from the world
Is my purity, my innocence, my inner little girl
Cuz sometimes right is wrong and wrong is right
Or life is death and death is life
And Nothing really is what is seems
But on another dimension, my access to truth
Comes to me in my dreams
God speaks to me and protects my soul
He whispers love songs to my spirit—can you hear it?
Nooooo!
Because He sings and dances with Me, and like a ballerina
He keeps me on my toes, allowing every move to naturally flow
And I smile
Cuz nobody knows about that secret hiding place
The one that lives inside of me
The one that makes me shout Jubilee
The one that lets me know, I'm free
Because it hides the little girl in me
But while that little girl hides, the woman in me seeks
The woman in me stands to her feet and is never afraid
To open her mouth and speak
The woman once broken and battered, but stronger than you think
She searches for wisdom and learns simplistic lessons
She basks in the midst of favor and shares her many blessings
But now the little girl that hides is ready to meet the woman that seeks
The two come together and they both equal **ME**.

1 Corinthians 2:10- these are the things God has revealed to us by his Spirit. The Spirit searches all things, even the deep things of God.

Romans 8:12-[12] Therefore, brothers and sisters, we have an obligation—but it is not to the flesh, to live according to it. [13] For if you live according to the flesh, you will die; but if by the Spirit you put to death the misdeeds of the body, you will live.

Deuteronomy 29:29-The secret things belong to the Lord our God, but the things revealed belong to us and to our children forever, that we may follow all the words of this law.

Jeremiah 23:24- Who can hide in secret places so that I cannot see them?"declares the Lord. "Do not I fill heaven and earth?"declares the Lord.

Proverbs 2:8- for he guards the course of the just and protects the way of his faithful ones.

Proverbs 2:11- Discretion will protect you, and understanding will guard you.

From My Journey to Yours

Forgiving

SHHHHH, just listen, I'm here to tell a story
It's amazing, and it's all about God's mercy and His glory
The other day I sat and thought about all the mistakes I made
But God quickly reminded me, that those things he already forgave
Then I thought about my life and how nothing seems to be fair
I heard the Lord say, "You're still breathing, aren't you my dear?"
I nodded gratefully and realized, how much I take for granted
And how thoughts can get twisted by simple word semantics
I remembered all the judgments and fingers pointing at me
He showed me the people pointing and how our spirits didn't agree
I was shown how my heart was hardened from years of wear and tear
He also showed me how afraid I was to show how much I cared
For people who have hurt me time and time again
I vowed to never let them in my life because I'm unforgiving
But God's answer was quite simple as he reminded me again
That I was already forgiven for all of my awful sin
So what gives me the right to judge or point my finger at someone else
When He forgave Me even when I couldn't forgive Myself
So my lesson learned today is that "existing" doesn't mean "I live"
And in order for me to live, I have to open my heart and forgive.

Ephesians 4:32- Be kind and compassionate to one another, forgiving each other, just as in Christ God forgave you.

Mathew 6:14- For if you forgive other people when they sin against you, your heavenly Father will also forgive you.

Matthew 18:21-22-Then Peter came to Jesus and asked, "Lord, how many times shall I forgive my brother or sister who sins against me? 22. Up to seven times?"Jesus answered, "I tell you, not seven times, but seventy-seven times.

1 John 1:9- If we confess our sins, he is faithful and just and will forgive us our sins and purify us from all unrighteousness.

From My Journey to Yours

_____

_____

_____

_____

_____

_____

_____

_____

_____

_____

A smile

Is a smile a reflection of one's souls and the secrets embedded in one's heart?
If so, my smile is afflicted and has been pierced with the point of a dart.
I think a smile symbolizes beauty, but it also shows one's pain
It speaks as the voice of one's soul, while it camouflages one's shame
When I look at the faces of people and see that they're missing a smile
I often wonder if it was stolen or lost, and if it's been gone for a while?

Job 9:27-If I say, 'I will forget my complaint, I will change my expression, and smile

Job 29:24-When I smiled at them, they scarcely believed it; the light of my face was precious to them

James 1:2-Consider it pure joy, my brothers and sisters, whenever you face trials of many kinds

Proverbs 15:13-15- A happy heart makes the face cheerful, but heartache crushes the spirit. 14. The discerning heart seeks knowledge, but the mouth of a fool feeds on folly. 15. All the days of the oppressed are wretched, but the cheerful heart has a continual feast.

From My Journey to Yours

Can You See Me?

Can you see me…I'm the child silenced in the darkness, who clings to life through hope--Hoping for brighter todays and even better tomorrows that my yesterdays have stolen away. Through my own pride, low self-esteem, and the insecurities of my own inadequacies—I learn early on to compensate my weaknesses by getting negative attention from men, while hoping to be acknowledged for my educational accomplishments and my ability to live past the standards set for most poverty stricken African American children…

Can you see me…I'm the pre-teen who's struggling with finding my voice in the world--The voice that was stolen with my innocence and buried in a hole of destitution. I hide behind anger and bitterness so I won't get hurt anymore and I lie to keep my secrets hidden so that no one will judge me and see my true shame. I look at others around me and wonder if they know what burdens have commanded my heart and held me captive for years…

Can you see me…I'm the teenager who's still searching for an identity because mine was chiseled away through physical abuse and sexual perversion. While longing for acceptance and validation, I retreat to my peers who are just as wounded and blind as I am. I allow my compassion for others to distort my understanding of loving and being loved by someone and then I learn that love is not love at all---its hate and then I learn to perfect it and I rebel…

Can you see me…I'm 19 years old with a hardened heart. I love to hate men because I know how to control them and I've mastered the art of using my beauty and sexuality. In every form of the word, I prostitute myself to get the things that make me happy. I love shopping and having nice things. But the more I take, the emptier my soul becomes and the further I drift into nothingness. I spiritually annihilate every man I can because the lust of their flesh disgusts me and has caused me to suffer for years…

Can you see me…I'm now the single mother who realizes that her mistakes in life don't have to continue-- I'm a survivor, I've survived through hardships in life, but it doesn't mean I use those hardships as an excuse to be cheated out of my own blessings. For every bit of neglect, abandonment, every beating and unauthorized touch I had to overcome—I've survived and am here to help others…

Can you see me…I'm a child of God who's been placed in a position to forgive myself and others who have hurt me…I am able to love, respect, and honor my mother and father even though they didn't always do the same for me. My heart has been turned back to God and he sees me…my strength, love, honesty, compassion, courage, intelligence, respect, selflessness, perseverance, and desire to live life righteously… So I ask again…Can you see me? Better yet, it doesn't matter what you can or can't see. The real question is…Can I see myself and the woman I am becoming in Christ? To God Be the Glory!

Jeremiah 29:11-For I know the plans I have for you," declares the Lord, "plans to prosper you and not to harm you, plans to give you hope and a future.

Romans 5:5- And hope does not put us to shame, because God's love has been poured out into our hearts through the Holy Spirit, who has been given to us.

Ephesians 4:26-"In your anger do not sin": Do not let the sun go down while you are still angry,

Psalms 37:8-Refrain from anger and turn from wrath; do not fret—it leads only to evil.

Romans 12:19-Do not take revenge, my dear friends, but leave room for God's wrath, for it is written: "It is mine to avenge; I will repay," says the Lord.

Ephesians 1:7-In him we have redemption through his blood, the forgiveness of sins, in accordance with the riches of God's grace

2 Corinthians 12:9-But he said to me, "My grace is sufficient for you, for my power is made perfect in weakness." Therefore I will boast all the more gladly about my weaknesses, so that Christ's power may rest on me.

Isaiah 40:3-but those who hope in the Lord will renew their strength. They will soar on wings like eagles; they will run and not grow weary, they will walk and not be faint.

From My Journey to Yours

Get Ready!!!

The power of love comes from within
Its strength can overpower any type of sin
We must get on our knees and pray, humble ourselves
It's not about outer beauty or the status of one's wealth
The spirit, soul, and flesh need peace
While confusion and turmoil are commanded to cease
By the voice of the I AM, one's shame is lifted
Through the abundance of the tares the wheat is being sifted
A chosen people have the promises from the Almighty Lord
Eternal Life is being birthed through the Lamb's bloodshed of the sword
His promises are kept and his spirit gives life
It's the church that he's coming back for-- to make His beautiful wife!!
Don't get left behind—we're at the zero hour
It's just a matter of time before you feel the Almighty's power.
Get Ready!!!

1 Thessalonians 4:16-18- For the Lord himself will come down from heaven, with a loud command, with the voice of the archangel and with the trumpet call of God, and the dead in Christ will rise first. After that, we who are still alive and are left will be caught up together with them in the clouds to meet the Lord in the air. And so we will be with the Lord forever. Therefore encourage one another with these words.

1 Corinthians 15:52- in a flash, in the twinkling of an eye, at the last trumpet. For the trumpet will sound, the dead will be raised imperishable, and we will be changed.

Luke 21:36- Be always on the watch, and pray that you may be able to escape all that is about to happen, and that you may be able to stand before the Son of Man."

Acts 17:30-31- In the past God overlooked such ignorance, but now he commands all people everywhere to repent. [31] For he has set a day when he will judge the world with justice by the man he has appointed. He has given proof of this to everyone by raising him from the dead."

From My Journey to Yours

_____

_____

_____

_____

_____

_____

_____

_____

_____

_____

_____

Nothing
(Double meaning)

I heard nothing, felt nothing, and accepted nothing
Because you said nothing, did nothing, and you gave nothing
So I learned to value nothing because I had nothing
I loved nothing because nothing loved me
I never gave up nothing because I had nothing to lose
I chased after nothing because I knew nothing
And, nothing consumed my life more than anything,
Because having nothing was better than accepting anything
I accepted knowing nothing, but I wanted to know something
So I was willing to let go of nothing for something
Knowing something helped me realize that nothing is worth losing for something.
Now I know something is better than nothing and I still won't accept just anything

Job 15:3- Would they argue with useless words, with speeches that have no value?

Proverbs 10:2- Ill-gotten treasures have no lasting value, but righteousness delivers from death.

1Timothy 6:7- For we brought *nothing* into the world, and we can take *nothing* out of it.

Isaiah 44:18- They know *nothing*, they understand *nothing*; their eyes are plastered over so they cannot see, and their minds closed so they cannot understand.

John 15:5- "I am the vine; you are the branches. If you remain in me and I in you, you will bear much fruit; apart from me you can do *nothing*

From My Journey to Yours

Betrayal

The Thief In the Night

You were welcome to come into my home uninvited
But I started to see how your intent ignited
A fire of hatred and bitterness that wanted to rape and molest my hidden innocence
That was untouched from those who already took from me
What I thought was my pride and my dignity
I believe you wanted to see me breakdown and lose all of my faith
But God's love is stronger for me than any diabolical hate
So I was finally given the vision to see
That you entered my home, not as my friend, but my enemy
Your intent was to steal whatever you wanted
While leaving my home broken and haunted
With your aura of fake love and devotion
While it concocted a lot of commotion
Like a thief in the night you came to steal kill and destroy
Knowing that your motives were a ploy
To break down and reject a home seeking true joy
I've always felt your jealousy and your desire to beat me down
Through my successes and accomplishments you smiled
But behind your smiles I saw the frown that judged me all day long
As you pointed your finger at all the things I've done wrong
You attack my character and my devotion as a mother
You defame my virtue and talk about me amongst each other
Wishing I was the person that you portrayed me to be
Knowing that your friendship was not real, but just an opportunity
To slither your way into a place of trust, while planning to
Destroy me with your authentic disgust
No you never told me directly how much you hate me
Instead you came as friend, even called yourself family
But I was finally given the vision to see
That you entered my home, not as my friend, but my enemy

So regardless of whether you came to steal, kill, and destroy
God's unconditional love protects my everlasting joy!

Psalm 41:19- Even my close friend, someone I trusted, one who shared my bread, has turned against me.

John 10:10-The thief comes only to *steal* and *kill* and destroy; I have come that they may have life, and have it to the full.

Job 15:34- For the company of the godless will be barren, and fire will consume the tents of those who love bribes.

Mathew 24:10- At that time many will turn away from the faith and will betray and hate each other

Romans 3:23- for all have sinned and fall short of the glory of God,

From My Journey to Yours

_____

_____

_____

_____

_____

_____

_____

_____

_____

Weapons

Some people use a gun or knife on the people they attack
But Y-O-U, you, you used your mouth to stab me in my back
I bet you wonder how that's possible, but your tongue is a two-edge blade
And you probably never thought your true colors would conveniently be displayed
Under the pressure you finally broke and tried to finish your assassination
Of a leader who intimidated your hate, with love, not confrontation
So your weapons were the words and the basis of your attacks
But my shield deflected your strikes, after the first stab in my back
No need to try to hide the weapons from the judge on judgment day
You made the choice to attack and there's a price that must be paid
To all the lives that's wounded with the knife you hid so well
Under your rotted flesh of hatred as it began to smell
So pungent and repulsive as if death was standing near
My body when your presence was in my atmosphere
Your attacks were quite brutal and could've killed me long ago
But God's protection over my life is what began to show
That with death comes resurrection and a much greater life
Of love and compassion to overpower anyone's anger or strife
Towards me as well as others who get silently attacked
But it's your mouth that became the knife that also stabbed them in their backs
But I thank you for your obedience to the father that you serve
Because he knew who to use and who would really have the nerve
To strike at the anointed lives who can threaten the evil kingdom
That robs the righteous of their inheritance and tries to strip away their freedom
To walk in love and redemption from the wounds your weapons caused
But God's perfection is exhibited in ALL imperfections and flaws
And your words can't harm anymore lives—You need to get to

stepp'in
Your bladed tongue is dull and no longer a deadly weapon.

Proverbs15:4- The soothing *tongue* is a tree of life, but a perverse *tongue* crushes the spirit.

Psalms 34:13- keep your *tongue* from evil and your lips from telling lies.

Proverbs 12:18- The words of the reckless pierce like swords, but the *tongue* of the wise brings healing.

Ephesians 4:29-Do not let any unwholesome talk come out of your mouths, but only what is helpful for building others up according to their needs, that it may benefit those who listen.+

Proverbs 17:20- One whose heart is corrupt does not prosper; one whose *tongue* is perverse falls into trouble.

Proverbs 21:23- Those who guard their mouths and their tongues keep themselves from calamity.

From My Journey to Yours

Unauthorized Touches

You put your hand on my face and grab me in violent way
You caress my arm and hold my hand as you ask me stay
In your presence for a little while
Because looking at me really makes you smile
And I agree-- not realizing what that decision is doing to me
Our time spent is one of a kind
Sitting down and talking wasn't on either of our minds
Yeah, we talked alright--with our bodies and communicated sexual sin
Then in my heart I'm crying because I'm repenting again
As I realize I'm allowing this temple of God to be defiled
But my spirit is too drawn in to break away because I'm in denial
About the feeling I have that sends a burning desire
That runs through my body like a hot scorching fire
I'm all messed up!!!
Not Knowing I'm allowing you an authorized touch
Of the vessel that God has chosen as His temple to live
And here I am giving away "me"—The one thing I shouldn't give
So…while the touching and intimacy made my body feel REAL good
My mind was battling with my flesh like a street fight in the hood
I thought unauthorized meant being raped or touched when I've already said, "no"
But I found out it also stop one's spiritual growth
Unauthorized can be a touch of molestation which is sexual abuse
It can be fornication and masturbation which are acts that denial tries to excuse
It's physical violence by someone who knows you can't defend yourself
Or taking on someone else's emotional stress while it wears on your own health
So the acts of being violated by ourselves or other's doesn't take much
Just remember what it means when you define an unauthorized touch

Hebrews 2:2- For since the message spoken through angels was binding, and every *violation* and disobedience received its just punishment,

1 John 5:17- All wrongdoing is *sin*, and there is *sin* that does not lead to death.

1 Corinthians 6:18- Flee from *sexual* immorality. All other sins a person commits are outside the body, but whoever sins sexually, sins against their own body.

Luke 11:4- Forgive us our sins, for we also forgive everyone who sins against us. And lead us not into temptation.

From My Journey to Yours

_____

_____

_____

_____

_____

_____

_____

_____

_____

_____

_____

A woman scorned

I saw you looking at me, and yeah I'm looking back
You're holding hands with your lady and still trying to be a Mack
You like what you see – am I soft on the eyes?
You look like you want something in between my thighs
Wait a minute now-I want you to open your mouth and tell me what you want from me
Oh you want me to be your booty call in between midnight and three?
I don't know, cause you got the potential for me to really like you
Nah, I can't mess with a dude that I think can possibly be my boo
Don't talk sweet, no need to front—You already established what you want
Well let me think, will you buy me stuff and take me out for drinks?
You said yes?-Alright it's a bet
Well all this time I've been used as a tool, don't make sense to try to break old rules
You're just like the rest-- there are no faithful men around
I might as well mess with you – at least I know what's going down
So what if your lady is at home holding down things
You're supposed to be at home too, not hiding your wedding ring
So why are you here with me, if you love your lady so much?
Oh-- you just need to feel a different woman's warm touch
I get it now…you're going do what I allow
If I let you have sex with me and treat me real foul
You'll keep the $$$ rolling and let me into your world
Eventually you'll let your boys know that I'm your side girl
Even in the streets females know what's up
But every now and then you get spiritually sucked
By the ecstacy of sin, not knowing the cost is greater than money
Then you come to my house to have sex with your so-called "sweetheart" and "honey"
And tell me that you love me and will always be around
The next day you hitt'in me in the face and throwing me on the ground
I was nothing to you from the day we first met
My kids have seen me go through the wringer and I've lost their

respect
Every abusive action you show me just wears my spirit thin
Not understanding what I'm creating through the torment of my own sin
In my heart, all I want is love and respect
But feeling in my mind the effects of abuse and neglect
Trying to hold on as I pray in silence
Asking God to get me out of this life of internal violence
So I decide to make a change to get my life right
No, I didn't know I would have to lose my life
Holding on to pain because I'm afraid of true peace
Giving in to unworthiness and holding on to grief
My burdens are heavy and mind is confused
But I'm ready to win—what more can I lose?
I've been held as a prisoner through blood, sweat, and tears
Now it's time to trade in these tears for hopeful new years
It is God's love and mercy that has kept me holding on
Cause I no longer want to live this life as another woman scorned

Romans 12:9-Love must be sincere. *Hate* what is evil; cling to what is good.

Deuteronomy 5:18-"You shall not commit *adultery*.

Ezekial 23:43-Then I said about the one worn out by *adultery*, 'Now let them use her as a prostitute, for that is all she is

Colossians 3:5-Put to death, therefore, whatever belongs to your earthly nature: *sexual immorality*, impurity, lust, *evil* desires and greed, which is idolatry.

Jude 1:7-In a similar way, Sodom and Gomorrah and the surrounding towns gave themselves up to *sexual immorality* and perversion. They serve as an example of those who suffer the punishment of eternal fire.

1 Corinthians 10:13-No temptation has overtaken you except what is common to mankind. And God is faithful; he will not let you be tempted beyond what you can bear. But when you are tempted, he will also provide a way out so that you can endure it.

From My Journey to Yours

Repentance

Whether it was love or lust—it doesn't matter today
Instead, I hope you get on your knees and take the time to pray
For the lives you affected and the souls you've broken
Not even taking the time to apologize as a token
Of remorse for the people who now grieve
Over the escapade of your lies and broken hearts you deceived
Through your string of conceived anger and malice
The devil rules the world as king and you live in his palace
But the truth came out just in the nick of time
Not knowing while I chose to ignore the signs
Of a man who I would normally NEVER have given the time of day
So it was destined that things turned out this way
While you were secretly having sex with two of us and being a freak
The truth just shows how desperate and weak
A man in a place of authority can really be
Because in your home you show your own insecurity
As you cause hurt, pain and calamity
So despite the tragedy of these foolish games
Blessings always come from the simplicity of one's pain
While I'm still healing from my own issues of insecurity
I'm blessed to know I don't share ties with your impurity
And I'll admit my ego and my spirit got broke
During the course of this situationship and its low hope
I knew I had to pray to God to get through
Because without a true heart of repentance who knows what God will do?

Jeremiah 31:19- After I strayed, I repented; after I came to understand, I beat my breast. I was ashamed and humiliated because I bore the disgrace of my youth.'

2 Corinthians 7:10- Godly sorrow brings *repentance* that leads to salvation and leaves no regret, but worldly sorrow brings death.

Mathew 3:8- Produce fruit in keeping with *repentance*.

Hebrews 6:1- Therefore let us move beyond the elementary teachings about Christ and be taken forward to maturity, not laying again the foundation of *repentance* from acts that lead to death, and of faith in God,

1 John 1:9- If we confess our sins, he *is* faithful and just and will forgive us our sins and purify us from *all* unrighteousness.

Ezekial 18:21- "But if a *wicked* person turns away from *all* the sins they have committed and keeps *all* my decrees and does what *is* just and right, that person will surely live; they will not die.

From My Journey to Yours

True Friend

Truth, Honesty, Loyalty, and Dedication
Should be basic characteristics of friendship, NOT forced expectations
But for some reason there was an error or mistake
That showed that our friendship was not real, but fake
It's unfortunate that knowledge of my pain
Was used as a way to conquer, win, or gain
Control of my heart through calculated words
In response to something I said-- based on what you "supposedly" heard
Instead of coming to me to verify if any of it was true
You defied the laws of friendship that were comfortable for you
And the deceit you spoke from your true heart turned out to be okay
Since a true friendship is never what you displayed to me any way
Your motives and defiance came out with revelations
That you lied to me about in previous conversations
And while it broke my heart to pieces, I can truly understand
Why our so-called friendship didn't survive uncomfortable demands
Like being compassionate and sympathetic while your friend faces his/her greatest fears
Or being understanding when one needs a listening heart, not listening ears
But general characteristics of a friend was what I thought I had in you
Until I found out you were the enemy who used friendship to disguise the truth
Of what you felt about me and my children, who I must add, you also hated
And instead of acknowledging it, it was my own feelings I negated
To avoid having to face the facts that I had to bear and grin
That you were never, to me, what I was to you—And that's a TRUE friend.

Proverbs 17:17- A *friend* loves at all times, and a brother is born for a time of adversity.

Proverbs 18:24- One who has unreliable friends soon comes to ruin, but there is a *friend* who sticks closer than a brother.

Job 16:20- My intercessor is my *friend* as my eyes pour out tears to God

Proverbs 12:26- The righteous choose their friends carefully, but the way of the wicked leads them astray.

Proverbs 16:28- A perverse person stirs up conflict, and a gossip separates close friends.

From My Journey to Yours

Deceit

The feeling of deceit is tormenting and makes one feel exposed
Especially when the deceiver is someone whose heart you think you know
The deceit is conceived in lies and malice, controlling through manipulation
It starts off with so-called truth and honesty, and loyal dedication
When the deceiver is exposed, his motives are no longer hidden or discreet
He doesn't show compassion or humility in the face of his own defeat
There is no positive spin to deception it simply shows the true reflection
Of one's insecurities and the need to control another's life
Bringing forth lies, hatred, bitterness, anger or strife
Leaving the victim feeling hopeless and unable to cope
But God is the healer and true revealer of truth, honesty and hope
Deceit is derived from negativity and the positives in life are only achieved
Through faith in God and not in man's infirmity
So if you're deceived, you must simply believe that God has already rewarded you
With a blessing of love sent from above and given from a place of truth!
NEVER DECEIT!

Proverbs 20:24- A person's steps are directed by the LORD. How then can anyone understand their own way?

2 Corinthians 5:2- For we must all appear before the judgment seat of Christ, so that each of us may receive what is due us for the things done *while* in the body, whether good or *bad*.

Proverbs 20:17- Food gained by fraud tastes sweet, but one ends up with a mouth full of gravel.

Psalms 120:2- Save me, Lord from lying lips and from deceitful tongues.

Psalms 5:6- you destroy those who tell lies. The bloodthirsty and deceitful you, Lord, detest.

From My Journey to Yours

Relationships

Possible Potential

Yeah, I said I loved you and that was real to me
But what I really loved was the man that you could possibly be
Potentially is the word I have to use
Because your love came in the form of a game and I could either win or lose
There was no in between and I see that now, but I wanted it and
It didn't matter when, where, or how—
Because you were potentially the man for me
You had everything I wanted and you said everything I wanted to hear
Even if what you said and did really wasn't sincere
Back then, I liked how you made me feel and I saw your ambition for success
Even if you wasn't there yet and your life was a big mess—
Yes, I settled and waited around because I could truly see
Even though you were broke and borrowed money from me
You were still a good looking man with possibility
You were sweet at times and partially dedicated to me
So if I stuck around "maybe" we "might" be a family
Does it sound crazy to you? Well it definitely sounds crazy to me
I was settling for something that had no certainty
Possibility is unverified, that means it's all tentative
You shouldn't have been in my world because "maybe's" were all you could give
I know I made it real easy for you to be important in my life
I guess I was just desperate to be someone's wife
While running around trying to make you a definite
Knowing full well that commitment is the #1 thing I won't get
From you or anyone else if I don't put certainty in my path
I look back at all the "maybe's" and then I simply laugh
At how angry I am at a man who is split in half
While struggling to be whole without submitting to the true and living God
And then I realize I'm wasting my time

Thinking about my future with a man who's a prisoner
and I'm paying the fines
Until I've had enough of being broke and battered
By the idea of having a man who really doesn't matter
One way or the other
Because he is just a brother
Who really can't be anything to me--
Other than a man with potential or possibility.

Hebrews 11:6- And without faith it is impossible to please God, because anyone who comes to him must believe that he exists and that he rewards those who earnestly seek him.

Mathew 19:26- Jesus looked at them and said, "With man this is impossible, but with God all things are possible."

Romans 8:7- The mind governed by the flesh is hostile *to God*; it does not *submit to* God's law, nor can it do so.

John 8:36- So if the Son sets you free, you will be free indeed.

Romans 10:3- Since they did not know the righteousness of God and sought to establish their own, they did not *submit* to God's righteousness.

From My Journey to Yours

Toxic Friendships

You don't have all the answers and yes you're misinformed
If you believe you have the right to tell me right from wrong
You have no claim or title to dictate my affairs
To others who are listening because you need a pair of ears
To listen to your gossip about everyone you know
"This one's marriage is breaking up", and "yeah girl she's a hoe"
Is that what you call friendship in this day and age?
Are you saying I should be honored to show the same colors you display?
In the group that you call friends, but talk about behind their backs
I should be honored and want to be a part of something like that?
I don't think so, you're mistaken if that's what friendship means to you
I may not be a perfect friend, but I can understand the clues
That point to a person who wants to make a believer
Out of people who choose to deal with the lies of a deceiver
While knowing it's a disguise to cover up the filthy ways
Of the nature of your friendships since high school and college days
You go right ahead and enjoy it, cuz it won't last forever
I'm glad to see that discernment makes me clever
To keep myself from the exposure of your so-called family group
Who only claimed to be my friends because I met them all through you
The one thing I have learned is that you must be evenly yoked
And I see our conflict because you're truly not my folks
I always knew our spirits were different--you said it's the colors I portrayed
When you conveniently let me know that my colors weren't the right shade
To be a part of what you called a great big family
That could only be classified as such if they took on your identity
I apologize if I offended your expectations of my dedication
But I'd much rather be in a coma or sedated on medication
Than to feel like I was obligated to live up to your expectations

Of loyalty and grace even when you spit directly in my face
Knowing that your ideas of the person you wanted me to be
Was only good enough to be in your group if I let you control me
And for a minute my brokenness labeled me as weak
So you played on my weakness and had an advantage over me
But I went back to my roots and was given authority
By the one who truly loves me and has the power to heal my heart
From a toxic friendship that never should've existed from the start

2 Corinthians 6:14- Do not be *yoked* together with unbelievers. For what do righteousness and wickedness have in common? Or what fellowship can light have with darkness?

Mathew 11:29- Take my *yoke* upon you and learn from me, for I am gentle and humble in heart, and you will find rest for your souls.

Romans 13:1- Let everyone be subject to the governing authorities, for there is no *authority* except that which God has established. The authorities that exist have been established by God.

From My Journey to Yours

The Rebound Chick

Me? A rebound chick? I don't think so…
I'm smart and beautiful—every man should know
I'm a hot commodity and men are knocking down my door,
They'd love to have me on their arm because I'm a good woman and more
I deserve to have a good man
And I don't need the headache of wondering where I stand
You tried to convince yourself, not me, that your ex wasn't a factor
But I'm sure you won your Oscar because you're a real good actor
You pulled me into your fantasy and made me believe a false reality
But you knew that I wasn't the person that you wanted in actuality
Instead you wanted your ex--the woman who broke you down
I was just the chick who helped you pick your ego up off the ground
Once you knew you could be desired, your self-esteem was uplifted
And it was me who had the screw face when your attention soon shifted
back to the woman who treated your heart like it was a joke
And when you went back her—you played yourself because there still wasn't any hope
You know she doesn't love you the same as she claims she did before
Especially each time she shows her ass and walks right out the door.
So again, I find it hard to accept the role I was played in
You decided to classify me-- as just a simple friend
Oh, you played the game—And you did it with a sweet and charming smile
But I guess you must've got tired after playing me for a while
However if you should, again, decide to keep a person bound
Remember that old saying "what goes around comes around"
So yeah, you did your dirt and it really makes me sick
To think that you could use me as your little rebound chick.

1 Thessalonians 5:18- *give* thanks in all circumstances; for this is God's will for you in Christ Jesus.

Ephesians 4:31- Get rid of all bitterness, rage and anger, brawling and slander, along with every *form* of malice.

Jeremiah 29:11- For I know the plans I have for you," declares the Lord, "plans to prosper you and not to harm you, plans to *give* you hope and a future.

From My Journey to Yours

Love to be loved

Am I beautiful to you?
The response is: I thought you knew.
Do you think I'm smart?
The response is: Come on, You're my heart.
Do you love me?
The response is: Baby, that's easy.
Each question I asked was never really answered
You evaded each one with a side-step, like a professional dancer
I **heard** what I wanted to **hear** because I love to be loved
And you were the one who affectionately gave me hugs
I had all of your attention and it felt so good to be seen
By a man who I imagined could be my king and I, his queen
I **believed** what I wanted to **believe** because I love to be loved
And you were the one who affectionately gave me hugs
It wasn't long before I had to pay for your affection
You acted like my security guard, but never used protection
To keep me guarded from the weapon you carried
While you was readily accepting all the benefits of us being married
Without actually accepting me as your legal wife
Showing me that you had no real commitment to stay in my life
But I **accepted** what I wanted to **accept** because I love to be loved
And you were the one who affectionately gave me hugs
Being in love with love can leave a person scarred
Because love is not worth having if you have to try real hard
To hear, believe, and accept a feeling that is given
And makes people feel so depressed they don't want to live in
A world filled with deceit and disguises love with an affectionate hug
And we make ourselves **hear, believe**, and **accept** it
Because we're in love with being in love...

1 John 3:18- Dear children, let us not love with words or speech but with actions and in truth.

Isaiah 5:20- Woe to those who call evil good and good evil, who put darkness for light and light for darkness, who put bitter for sweet and sweet for bitter.

Deuteronomy 13:3- you must not listen to the words of that prophet or dreamer. The Lord your God is testing you to find out whether you *love* him with all your heart and with all your soul.

Psalms 12:2- Everyone *lies* to their neighbor; they flatter with their lips but harbor deception in their hearts.

2 Timothy 2:22- Flee the evil desires of youth and pursue righteousness, faith, *love* and peace, along with those who call on the Lord out of a pure heart.

From My Journey to Yours

_____

_____

_____

_____

_____

_____

_____

_____

_____

_____

Heart Guardian

I submitted myself to you because I thought you truly cared
I let down my guard with you even though I still felt scared
You told me you'd protect me from the hurt and pain in life
I believed you and wanted to heal myself before I became your wife
I left my guarded heart wide open and wanted to let it all out
My pain, anguish and fears-- and all of my self-doubt
You listened and you heard me, at times you made me feel secure
But the pain inside my heart was too much for me to endure
You were supposed to guard my heart and keep it safe from harm
Instead, you were the one who set off my alarms
You stole my trust and treated me as if you didn't care
But because you were unhappy you felt your actions were justified and fair
I believed you'd protect me and be my strength when I was weak
I believed you'd be my eyes when I was blinded and couldn't see
But when all is said and done I have to thank you for your presence
All the mistakes you made and the promises un-kept showed me your true essence
A man of God is not doubled minded and unstable in all his ways
He walks with the Lord and seeks direction to make it through his days
While I point the finger of blame, I have to realize my own mistakes
You were only what I wanted you to be while I doubted my own faith
The position that I placed you in was wrong and now I see
You were not meant to guard my heart, but just to be a friend to me
Since I blamed you for my pain and rejection, as well as abandonment
I have to apologize and truly thank you for the time that we have spent
As a result of our relationship, my heart desires deliverance and peace
Now I see my true Heart Guardian is the one who brings me ease
It's the Holy Spirit inside me that dwells
And as my true Heart Guardian, The Holy Spirit NEVER fails!!

Proverbs 16:9-In their hearts humans plan their course, but the Lord establishes their steps.

Philippians 4:1- I can do all this through him who gives me strength.

Psalms 91:1- Whoever dwells in the shelter of the Most High will rest in the shadow of the Almighty.

Psalms 18:2- The Lord is my rock, my fortress and my deliverer; my God is my rock, in whom I take refuge, my shield and the horn of my salvation, my stronghold.

From My Journey to Yours

New Dog–Old Tricks!

You only see my external appearance and its appealing to your eyes
Do you like my pretty face, small waist, and big voluptuous thighs?
You say you want to take care of me, what makes you want to do that?
I have three kids, I'm a single mom-- can you handle those two facts?
I've heard that line a million times, what makes you different from the rest?
Are you sure you're ready for all of this, lets put you to the test
I'd like to wait until I'm married to be intimate again
Can you handle being in my life—only as a platonic friend?
I'm a praying woman, a woman who worships the True and Living God
How do feel about that, do you think it's kind of odd?
Have you ever hit a woman or called her out of her name?
Do you respect women enough, not to play silly childish games?
These are questions I have to ask, but I don't expect to get the truth.
You answered every single question right, but you must know I'm not a fool
The last three guys that approached me also answered all the questions right
It's amazing how the answers just flowed, not one of you put up a fight
While you played the game intelligently, you weren't totally prepared
You missed the insight I was given, so you were easily compared
To all the rest of the guys and yes you each have different names
But you look alike to me because your spirits are the same
I have to giggle because its funny and I really get a kick
Out of seeing the new dogs play the devil's old tricks.

1 John 4:- Dear friends, do not believe every spirit, but test the spirits to see whether they are from God, because many false prophets have gone out into the world.

1 Corinthians 1:19-"I will destroy the wisdom of the wise; the intelligence of the intelligent I will frustrate."

Ecclesiastes 1:9- What has been will be again, what has been done will be done again; there is *nothing new under* the sun

2 Corinthians 11:3-But I am afraid that just as Eve was deceived by the serpent's cunning, your minds may somehow be led astray from your sincere and pure devotion to Christ.

1 Peter 5:8- Be alert and of sober mind. Your enemy the devil prowls around like a roaring lion looking for someone to devour.

From My Journey to Yours

I See You!

My walls of armor with a fortress of fear
Kept everyone away who didn't belong here
But my heart longed and ached for a refuge of protection
And in the shadow of your wings came acceptance, not rejection
So as different as we may be and as different as we are,
Today and forever ever you are my shining star
Your heart is so genuine, your words so sincere
Even when you're not speaking, your voice sounds so clear
I hear it in your actions, your sacrifices your touch
And for this handicapped heart, your love became crutch
One that supports, commits, respects and adores
The person that I was, am, and will be as I walk with the Lord...
I want you to know that I see you
I see that your love is unconditional
And your expectations of me, are reasonable
You love me for who I am and accept all my flaws
And you never arrest my heart by breaking God's Love Laws
Your patience and willingness to accept who I am
Helps me to understand that I'm specially fashioned
Created and molded with intricate perfection
Designed by God for you...Keeping our souls connected
I want you to know that I see you
I see your heart, your motives, your fruitful tree
The one that grows fruit of love that nourishes ONLY me
I hear the passion inside of you that whispers to my soul
I'm the one who completes you, but its God who made you whole
I know that you see me and I see you too.
So I celebrate this love because I only have eyes for you
I see you!

Ephesians 6:11- [11] Put on the full armor of God, so that you can take your stand against the devil's schemes.

From My Journey to Yours

Parenting

A Single Mother's Cry

I'm crying out for help to be the best mother I can be
Raising my children alone is such a great responsibility
Especially in this day and age, when challenges come my way
I can only get on my knees and pray, while thanking the Lord each day
For the wisdom and the strength He has imparted in my heart
So I don't get discouraged on the paths that seem to end before they start
I get tired of the sacrifices that I always have to make
And I'm tired of hiding my pain through the smiles I have to fake
My spirit is crying out for some help and just a little peace
Because I'm shackled by my loneliness and I want to be released
Into the arms of a man of God who would love me and my girls
With no reservations about having a ready-made family in his world
In the past I made the mistake of dating men who were simply "nice"
When I should've focused more on whether they were submitted to Jesus Christ
So today I pay the price of making quick and hasty decisions
And being blinded by the loneliness that stopped my perfect vision
From seeing the true motives of men who weren't right for me
And never could've accepted being the head of my Christian family
Today I pray God's will for my life and I know he will provide
All my needs because he hears the sorrow of this single mother's cry.

Psalm 18:6-In my distress I called to the Lord; I cried to my God for help. From his temple he heard my voice; my cry came before him, into his ears.

Psalm 102-A prayer of an afflicted person who has grown weak and pours out a lament before **the Lord**.

Hear my prayer, **Lord**; let my **cry** for help come **to** you.

From My Journey to Yours

_____

_____

_____

_____

_____

_____

_____

_____

_____

_____

_____

Help Me!!!

Okay, right now I'm in a slump and my bills are sky high
The other day I was so stressed out I just broke down and cried
No food in the fridge and my washer and dryer don't work
My phone just got turned off and my heat and air just broke
I have three mouths to feed and I'm holding on to hope
I'm frustrated and tired--I'm at the end of my rope
But I can't give up I'm too strong for that and my life is just beginning
These situations and circumstances are temporary, I have to believe I'm winning
I refuse to let my life just worthlessly slip away
I'm given a chance to get it right when He wakes me up everyday
But my decisions in life are unstable and I'm left without a clue
Trying to figure out a mystery, looking for the moral thing to do
Let me get my life right and become renewed in my mind
God please help me overcome, never to come back to things so unkind
Hold onto my faith and let me walk with the divine
Never to revisit this shady, desolate past that should've never been mine
I'm begging and pleading, crying out from my soul
Lord please give me strength, restore me—make me whole!!
It's time and I coming with a broken and contrite heart
And you said you'd restore those of us who are ready for a new start
I'm praying and fasting and reading the bible everyday-- hoping you'll
Impart, in me, the wisdom that will help me find my way
Into your arms held safely and secure with your love
Knowing all I need is your protection sent from above
God you said if I hunger and thirst for righteousness that I would be filled
Does that also mean if I'm hurting that my pain will be healed?
I need you and I need you more and more each day
You know my heart and you see that I'm trying to find my way
While I struggle and I debate whether I should take the easy way out

I remember all of your promises and it takes away my doubts
I'm holding on because I know that help is on the way
My heart is pouring out all the things I want say
Yes…I trust You and love You and really want to stay
In your presence so that no one and nothing can hinder my spiritual growth
I'm crying like a baby wanting you to know
I'm not just an ordinary Christian putting on a show
My heart is in this war, I walk alone—it's no us
I'm not just another soldier taking orders-- I'm a warrior with purpose.
Help Me!!!

Philippians 4:11-13 [11] I am not saying this because I am in need, for I have learned to be content whatever the circumstances. [12] I know what it is to be in need, and I know what it is to have plenty. I have learned the secret of being content in any and every situation, whether well fed or hungry, whether living in plenty or in want. [13] I can do all this through him who gives me strength.

1 Corinthians 10:13- No temptation has overtaken you except what is common to mankind. And God is faithful; he will not let you be tempted beyond what you can bear. But when you are tempted, he will also *provide* **a way out so that you can endure it.**

Jeremiah 17:7-"But blessed is *the* **one who trusts** *in the Lord*, whose confidence is *in* **him.**

Psalms 18:35- You make your saving *help* **my shield, and your right hand sustains me; your** *help* **has made me great.**

Isaiah 41:10- So *do* not fear, for I am with you; *do* not be dismayed, for I am your God. I will strengthen you and *help* you; I will uphold you with my righteous right hand.

From My Journey to Yours

Sweet Baby Girls

I see the strength in your eyes, and your determination to grow
Into virtuous women of God, so you'll seek wisdom and you know
The path of righteousness dwells deep in your hearts
It's the straight and narrow path that sets you apart
From other little girls who think they truly know
But have no idea of your sacrifices and the maturity of your growth
I know it's hard to find your place in this world
But just remember you're mommy's sweet baby girls
Our lives are tough right now, but our struggles aren't in vain
Because nothing worth having, doesn't come with a little pain
But through perseverance and faith comes great strength
That enables us to endure through great lengths
And it doesn't matter if some days we don't get along
The love we share and our struggles keep our family bond strong
It's the cycle we must go through in order to survive and
While thanking God for another day that He's keeping us alive
Is just one part of our journey as we continue down the road
Of discovering the life God has for us as it begins to unfold
Your destiny has already been written and now it must be fulfilled
Because the strength in each of you has already been instilled
And I know it's hard to find your place in this world
Just remember you're mommy's sweet baby girls
I'm here for you through times that are good and bad
And even though, we're not a couple, so is your dad
Continue to ask questions and be the genius's that you are
Always do your best and keep reaching for the stars
You see, nothing is impossible or unable to obtain
Failure and disappointments can try to make you go insane
But God's glory and honor are given to
Sierra, Aniya, and Jaida-- you're all my beautiful pearls
God couldn't have blessed me with a better bunch of sweet baby girls.

Romans 8:28- And we know that in all things God works for the good of those who love him, who have been called according to his *purpose*.

John 16:33- I have told you these things, so that in me you may have peace. In this world you will have trouble. But take heart! I have overcome the world."

Ephesians 1:11- In him we were also chosen, having been *predestined* according to the plan of him who works out everything in conformity with the purpose of his will,

2 Timothy 1:9-He has saved us and called us to a holy life—not because of anything we have done but because of his own *purpose* and grace. This grace was given us in Christ Jesus before the beginning of time,

From My Journey to Yours

The Bigger Me!!

I'm growing up with my children, I'm bigger can't you see?
I've been learning to count my blessings
While humbly accepting life's lessons
I also want to thank my mom and dad
For loving me unconditionally with all they had
But my Jesus is great—He treats me real nice
I'll keep Him in my heart for the rest of my life
I enjoy growing and maturing, and I can't wait to see
What next year has in store for the brand new bigger me!

1 Peter 2:2- Like newborn *babies*, crave pure spiritual milk, so that by it you may grow up in your salvation,

2 Peter 3:18- But *grow in the* grace and knowledge of our *Lord* and Savior Jesus Christ. To him be glory both now and forever! Amen.

Ephesians 4:15- Instead, speaking *the* truth *in* love, we will *grow* to become *in* every respect *the* mature body of him who is *the* head, that is, Christ.

From My Journey to Yours

_____

_____

_____

_____

_____

_____

_____

_____

_____

_____

_____

You are not my father

Please don't leave me, what am I going to do?
You told me that you loved me and I thought your love was true
I found myself debating whether you fulfilled my life in truth
Then I wondered if you just filled a void that was emptied in my youth.
You see my father didn't raise me and I needed his guidance through the years
My mother left him when I was three years old, I guess she thought I didn't care
But a little girl needs her father for simple things you see
A father is a hero in the eyes of a small child, especially at age three
I use to sit and wonder if my father even loved me
I wrote him letters and sent him pictures just in case he wanted to see
If I had his eyes or a smile like his and if he still wanted me
I asked God if I'd ever see him or if he'd reappear
But my life continued without him and I accepted his absence through the years
My feelings of abandonment and rejection showed its ugly face
I didn't want a committed relationship for fear of being displaced
I missed the hugs and kisses while being daddy's little girl
Now I'm all grown up, looking for my daddy in this world
Fortunately I haven't found him and I know the reason why
The father I've always longed for has been right before my eyes
My father is in heaven and He will supply my needs
I just have to be obedient to His word and constantly take heed.
So while you gave me the hugs and kisses I've always wanted as a kid
You can never be my father or fix the hurt I've always hid
The voids I've tried to fill and the hurt I've tried to conceal
have tormented my soul and hindered my process to heal.
As my companion, I never expected my daddy issues to be such a bother
But I understand your frustration, with me, because you are NOT my father.

Ephesians 1:5 - God decided in advance to adopt us into his own family by bringing us to himself through Jesus Christ. This is what he wanted to do, and it gave him great pleasure.

Romans 8:15 - So you have not received a spirit that makes you fearful slaves. Instead, you received God's Spirit when he adopted you as his own children. Now we call him, "Abba, Father."

Ephesians 6 - Children, obey your parents because you belong to the Lord, for this is the right thing to do. "Honor your father and mother." This is the first commandment with a promise: If you honor your father and mother, "things will go well for you, and you will have a long life on the earth." ...

From My Journey to Yours

_____

_____

_____

_____

_____

_____

_____

_____

_____

_____

_____

_____

The LOVE poem

Love is kind, it's gentle, and honest
Love is forgiving, compassionate and flawless
Love is meek and humble, but strong and debonair
It's the feeling of completeness that keeps you floating on the air
Love is sacrifice and selflessness, stern and upright
It's knowing that you've found the one who saves your blindness with His sight
While it's perfect and unfailing it can leave you down and out
Sometimes LOVE can be complicated when one wallows in self-doubt
While love is classified as an emotion, it's plain and simple to see
Love is the Almighty, it's God presence in you and me.

1 Corintians:13 Three things will last forever—faith, hope, and love—and the greatest of these is love.

Numbers 14:18- The Lord is slow to anger and filled with unfailing love, forgiving every kind of sin and rebellion. But he does not excuse the guilty.

1 Chronicles 16:34

Give thanks to the Lord, for he is good! His faithful love endures forever.

John 15:9 - I have loved you even as the Father has loved me. Remain in my love.

John 3:16 - "For this is how God loved the world: He gave his one and only Son, so that everyone who believes in him will not perish but have eternal life.

From My Journey to Yours

A Borrowed Blessing
(dedicated to Baby Zaria)

A baby's life purpose is given before it's conceived
In the womb of a mother who truly believes
That God's love is perfect and He makes no mistakes
So we accept what He gives us because His wisdom is great
Accepting the gift of life can be challenging at times
Especially when "life" means the flesh won't survive
Such thoughts capture the heart and keep it confined
But the true test of love starts in the heart, not the mind
Sweet baby, you're released in spirit and in truth
Into the presence of the Lord—because He knows what's best for you
Oh yes, I'd love to see you grow up so I can kiss your sweet face
But I know you're laughing and dancing in a much better place
Of peace and serenity that I have never known
But look forward to experiencing when it's my time to come home
I send you with love and warm hugs and kisses
Because it's my spirit that rejoices, but my flesh that wishes
God's divine purpose for your life could be with me
Growing, playing, and having sibling rivalry
But never being forgotten is the priceless gift you've given
To each one of us, because we know you're in heaven
Baby girl—Spread your wings and fly as high as you can
Above the earth and the clouds and cities built by man
Baby, hear this message—It's important for you to know
Your spirit is free because I have to let go
And give back to the Lord – A blessing unselfishly
Borrowed with love and returned thankfully!!

Romans 14:8- If we *live*, we *live* for *the Lord*; and if we die, we die for *the Lord*. So, whether we *live* or die, we *belong to the Lord*.

Deuteronomy 29:29- *The* secret things *belong to the Lord* our *God*, but *the* things revealed *belong to* us and *to* our children forever, that we may follow all *the* words of this law.

Romans 15:13- May the God of hope fill you with all joy and peace as you trust in him, so that you may overflow with hope by the power of the *Holy Spirit*.

Psalms 139:13- For you created my inmost being; you knit me together in my mother's womb

From My Journey to Yours

Acknowledgment

This Experience

In your eyes I saw truth...I believed your loyalty as you showed me your hearts longings

In your voice was a melodious honesty that sang sweet love songs to my soul

Your gentle touch pierced my skin with a hot fiery passion of genuine sincerity and I gave in to all of your devices and surrendered, to you, all of my belongings

You see, my heart longed and ached for such affection and you were the only person who penetrated my shield enough to touch the true essence of my secret desires and the mysteries they held

I spoke no words of affirmation and I divulged no secrets of my hidden scars until you showed me that you were not my enemy...and I could trust you.

I welcomed you into my home and allowed you to share time and space with me and my daughters...you consumed food that I not only prepared with my hands, but included my heart as an ingredient and it was ingested by you each time you nourished your body

I submitted to you the sweet nectar of my femininity as I shared with you the deepest part of my sexual passion in seductive truth.

I divulged, to you, every part of me that there was and you accepted it—knowing that the responsibility was great and you were unworthy of receiving it....

As I reflect on this experience, I thank you for your purpose in my life. Had I not felt such a deep, tender affection like the one I thought we shared...I never would've seen my true blessing in this experience...

Before you, I was certain that I had been stripped of my Nubian essence because my core had been damaged from repeated acts of sodomy and forceful acts of sexual molestation that had stripped away the vibrant life that existed inside me...

This experience shows me that I have a love inside of me that's greater than the hate that has been conceived through my wounds and that I can love with intensity and compassion, limitlessly.

This experience...shows me that there is no time and space for true love and that people assign those roles to what and how long love should take to be originated in our hearts, but I am an exception to that rule because I realize that there's no true timeframe of love that exists in this time and space outside of our own realities

This experience.... has hurt me, but I will also heal from it and learn that life is a process of hurting, healing, and learning. And I gain the knowledge that's necessary to survive and then I do...now I see the value of life and the importance of "love"—not as an emotion but as a state of being in God...so this experience has shown me that love conquers all because God conquers all ...and so I bow out gracefully and I thank you for this experience.

1 Corinthians 6:13- You say, "Food for the stomach and the stomach for food, and God will destroy them both." The body, however, is not meant for sexual immorality but for the Lord, and the Lord for the body.

2 Timothy 1:9- He has saved us and called us to a holy life—not because of anything we have done but because of his own *purpose* and grace. This grace was given us in Christ Jesus before the beginning of time

1 John 4:16- And so we know and rely on the love God has for us. God is love. Whoever lives in love lives in God, and God in them.

Ephesians 3:19- [19] and to know this love that surpasses knowledge—that you may be filled to the measure of all the fullness of God.

2 Corinthians 7:10-[10] Godly sorrow brings repentance that leads to salvation and leaves no regret, but worldly sorrow brings death.

From My Journey to Yours

The Courage to love

You kissed me tenderly and always held me close
I welcomed your sweet touch because you knew I needed it the most
Growing up without love, kept me guarded for years
But I showed you the true me and never held back my tears
I even had secret desires that I wanted only you to see
I remember feeling loved and cherished every time you kissed me
I didn't realize my fear of true love was all bottled up inside
So I struggled with the thoughts of your denial and your lies
You always tried to convince me that your heart truly loved me
But in actuality I was a rebound chick that was in you life conveniently
I remember all the talks we had...yeah I was really number one
In reality you was just looking for a place to run and hide
Were you trying to take my virtue and break my ego and my pride?
Our relationship wasn't about love, I believe you just wanted sex
And was looking for a sista to help you get back at your ex
But for me you see I loved you and it wasn't an easy task
I'll admit to being afraid and secretly wearing a mask
But I truly opened myself up to a feeling that I couldn't shake
I even pinched myself from time to time to see if I was awake
No...I wasn't dreaming and yes you hurt me more than you know
It was your actions not your words that truly began to show
That the love I reluctantly began to nurture in honesty and truth
Should've remained mysterious and hidden and never should've seen the likes of you
But I'm grateful and now I know the Man from up above
Only had you in my life to show me that I have the courage to love

Romans 12:9- ⁹Love must be sincere. Hate what is evil; cling to what is good.

Romans 8:28- ²⁸ And we know that in all things God works for the good of those who love him, who[a] have been called according to his purpose.

Isaiah 26:10- But when grace is shown to the wicked, they do not learn righteousness; even in a land of uprightness they go on doing evil and do not regard the majesty of the Lord.

Joshua 1:9- Have I not commanded you? Be strong and courageous. Do not be afraid; do not be discouraged, for the Lord your God will be with you wherever you go."

From My Journey to Yours

And it works'

Don't want to flatter myself into thinking I'm something I'm not
But if I had to make a bet, I'd say you want something I've got
Your eyes crave the first sign of sin
Satisfying your inner desires and then here comes that grin
You take possession of a thought that's foul and rotten
Thinking about our bodies entangled on fresh sheets of Egyptian cotton
Then you manipulate Love's seduction with "flattery" as a disguise
To get what you want in between my thighs
And it works!-Temporarily.
Depositing your coins of destruction into the bank of my heart
And in my broken dysfunction, I find it hard to love smart
Now pieces of me float around, fragmented and impaired
And I'm barely existing in a poverty stricken atmosphere
My vision is poor—I see hazy!
Too afraid to work hard, so I spend time being lazy
And like a beggar on the street, I shake my cup to get fed
Don't even need a whole meal, I'll take one slice of bread
Because I'm starving—Spiritually
Even tempted to let my heart grow cold
But deep down inside God only knows
That I struggle with the option to love or to hate
So I disconnect my heart—That's how I feel safe
And it works!--Temporarily.
Til I learn that wisdom extends far beyond my days in college
And that true love can abound more and more in my heart
But only thru God's knowledge
So I turn to a place that will help my heart to discern
That love is a "state of being" and cannot be learned
I accept God's promises as a guaranteed deposit of what's to come
And there's only one place I can get it from
And that's the Holy Spirit
I'm in a relational mess and I must confess—I'm worn out
And getting a "FALSE" sense of love in all the right places
While seeking approval from all the wrong faces

Just keeps me digesting the poison of seduction
Which minimizes the power in me to accept a healthy production
Of smart love, with a smart heart, giving me the chance for a brand new start
 And accepting new deposits with shiny coins of protection
That fills my heart's bank with God's love blessing
Then I live well and love well
And it works! Permanently!

James 3:17- But the wisdom that comes from heaven is first of all pure; then peace-loving, considerate, submissive, full of mercy and good fruit, impartial and sincere.

Proverbs 4:6- Do not forsake wisdom, and she will protect you; love her, and she will watch over you.

James 1:12-16- [12] Blessed is the one who perseveres under trial because, having stood the test, that person will receive the crown of life that the Lord has promised to those who love him.

[13] When tempted, no one should say, "God is tempting me." For God cannot be tempted by evil, nor does he tempt anyone; [14] but each person is tempted when they are dragged away by their own evil desire and enticed. [15] Then, after desire has conceived, it gives birth to sin; and sin, when it is full-grown, gives birth to death.

[16] Don't be deceived, my dear brothers and sisters.

Mark 14:38- Watch and pray so that you will not fall into temptation. The spirit is willing, but the flesh is weak."

James 1:12- Blessed is the one who perseveres under trial because, having stood the test, that person will receive the crown of life that the Lord has promised to those who love him.

1 Corinthians 6:18-20- Flee from sexual immorality. All other sins a person commits are outside the body, but whoever sins sexually, sins against their own body. [19] Do you not know that your bodies are temples of the Holy Spirit, who is in you, whom you have received from God? You are not your own; [20] you were bought at a price. Therefore honor God with your bodies.

From My Journey to Yours

Why? Is a question that explores the depth of truth
Why? Gives an answer that helps fragments to re-group
Why? Answers the questions to help bring forth closure
Why? Often reveals hurt and ultimate exposure
Of people who aren't truthful about the thoughts that enter their minds
Why? Also gives one a solution of <u>why</u> one should leave the past behind
Why? Can answer questions that leave your mind confused
Why? Will give the answer that can bring about Good News
Why is an important question because it often reveals the hidden
Contents of a person and also shows what's driven
In the heart of those we question because the When's, What's, and How's
Are not enough to answer **why** we need to make important decisions now.

Proverbs 2:6- For the Lord gives wisdom, from his mouth come knowledge and understanding.

Proverbs 3:5-6- Trust in the Lord with all your heart and lean not on your own understanding; ⁶ in all your ways submit to him, and he will make your paths straight.

James 1:6- But when you ask, you must believe and not doubt, because the one who doubts is like a wave of the sea, blown and tossed by the wind.

Proverbs 9:10- The fear of the Lord is the beginning of wisdom, and knowledge of the Holy One is understanding.

Ephesians 1:17- I keep asking that the God of our Lord Jesus Christ, the glorious Father, may give you the Spirit of wisdom and revelation, so that you may know him better.

From My Journey to Yours

A Queen
(my affirmation)

This morning I woke up and realized I've always been a queen
I looked in the mirror and saw royalty and no it wasn't a dream
I don't have to fantasize and glamorize about what I want to be
The honor has already been assigned and given unto me
I'm regal and suave-my heritage is strong
I sit on a throne because that's where I belong
I don't need your affirmations to see the value of my life
And I don't want to be a broken battered or empty-souled wife
Who told you that love means I have to be your slave?
My shackles have been cut and I'm no longer willing to trade
My self- respect, identity, or pennies for my wealth
But most importantly, I devalued all of my own worth
While being destined to prosper since the day of my birth
It's not my fault that you're a man who doesn't love or respect himself
I'm not your mirror so you can reflect your abusive ways onto me
I prefer God uses His light to blind every dark part that I can't see
Now what I'm saying should not be taken as me being mean
I just simply needed to tell you, you're in the presence a queen
Remember that!

1 Peter 2:9- ⁹ But you are a chosen people, a royal priesthood, a holy nation, God's special possession, that you may declare the praises of him who called you out of darkness into his wonderful light.

Deuteronomy 14:2- ² for you are a people holy to the Lord your God. Out of all the peoples on the face of the earth, the Lord has chosen you to be his treasured possession.

John 15:16- ¹⁶ You did not choose me, but I chose you and appointed you so that you might go and bear fruit—fruit that will last—and so that whatever you ask in my name the Father will give you.

Matthew 5:48- ⁴⁸ Be perfect, therefore, as your heavenly Father is perfect.

From My Journey to Yours

_____

_____

_____

_____

_____

_____

_____

_____

_____

_____

Choices

Hallelujah means the highest praise
And to you Lord, my hands are raised
I eagerly anticipate an answer or reflection
Of your voice pointing me in the right direction
But I can't hear you now because I'm too far away
As I made the choice this morning –not to stop and pray
The struggle is way too much to bear
As I hear the enemy whisper in my ear
That I'm too weak to be on the front line
To fight with the righteous and walk with the divine
I digress—I'm here to make a choice
I desire to hear the commandments of your voice
Because my heart is longing for the intimacies
That we shared days on end—just you and me
Now I'm struggling to fight-- just to stay free
From the clutches of the pain that centers in my brain
Holding me captive as I go insane
I can't take it no more and I give in to a migraine
That debilitates my functions and desire to fight
Against what has held me captive all of my life
I'm struggling with the fear of the greatness you've given
To the flesh that I walk in, but it's my heart that's driven
By Your word and your commandment to set me free
From the strongholds that I once gave to the enemy
So I seek your face and cry out in prayer
"There's no room for you devil—not in here!!"
Lord please give me strength?—I need to hear your voice
I'm down on my knees because I've made my choice.
Let's pray!!

Romans 8:35- ³⁵ Who shall separate us from the love of Christ? Shall trouble or hardship or persecution or famine or nakedness or danger or sword?

Colossians 1:20-22- [20] and through him to reconcile to himself all things, whether things on earth or things in heaven, by making peace through his blood, shed on the cross.

[21] Once you were alienated from God and were enemies in your minds because of[a] your evil behavior. [22] But now he has reconciled you by Christ's physical body through death to present you holy in his sight, without blemish and free from accusation—

2 Samuel 14:14- [14] Like water spilled on the ground, which cannot be recovered, so we must die. But that is not what God desires; rather, he devises ways so that a banished person does not remain banished from him.

From My Journey to Yours

Mistakes

What are life's lessons, how do we know?
What makes us who we are and how do we grow
To be responsible and make the best decisions
Or make right, our wrongs with complete revisions?
Our mistakes are life lessons used to nurture our growth
So opportunities aren't passed and missing all hope
We are human beings and we make mistakes that help to keep us grounded
We can only strive for perfection and search our own hearts for the unfounded
We receive our strength from God to make it through the storm
He covers and protects us to keep us safe from harm
While mistakes can't always be repaired
The experiences can be shared
So stay focused, and always remember your mistakes are simple gifts
They're similar to life jackets that helps one to stay adrift
Mistakes are God's way of training us for life
They help in times of blindness by giving us back our sight
Hold on to your holiness and let your errors keep you in the spiritual fight
Instead release your mistakes knowing you're being chastened in God's light

James 3:2- 2 We all stumble in many ways. Anyone who is never at fault in what they say is perfect, able to keep their whole body in check.

2 Timothy 3:16-17- 16 All Scripture is God-breathed and is useful for teaching, rebuking, correcting and training in righteousness, 17 so that the servant of God[a] may be thoroughly equipped for every good work.

Isaiah 41:10- So do not fear, for I am with you; do not be dismayed, for I am your God.

I will strengthen you and help you; I will uphold you with my righteous right hand.

Ephesians 6:12- 12 For our struggle is not against flesh and blood, but against the rulers, against the authorities, against the powers of this dark world and against the spiritual forces of evil in the heavenly realms.

1 John 1:9-If we confess our sins, he is faithful and just and will forgive us our sins and purify us from all unrighteousness.

From My Journey to Yours

Redemption

Healing

I look in the mirror and see that my scars are beginning to heal
A cut on my arm and a burn here and there were frighteningly all too real
Marks of abuse and anger that left my heart hard as stone
Because I've always tried to deal with pain of these wounds all alone
So the deepest cut on my body was right in the middle of my heart
All mangled and torn to shreds were the most delicate of all the parts
So I asked the Lord to honor His word that He has often revealed
That enables most wounded sinners the option to be spiritually healed
My healing is miraculous when I look at how the scars disappear
My wounds are not recognizable as if they were never even here
At times I can see a remnant of what the wounds left behind
But I'm no longer tormented by lacking serenity and peace of mind
I thank the Lord abundantly for His grace and mercy bestowed
On the back of an awful sinner who's been carrying such a heavy load
Of lies, deceit and fornication against my own body and soul
The vessel that God is using to be made virtuous and whole
And the fragments of my brokenness keep me reminded everyday
Of the path of righteousness He created to help all of us find our way
Into a relationship of love and commitment that will always begin to reveal
That God is the Almighty power that enables each one of us to heal

Proverbs 12:18-The words of the reckless pierce like swords, but the tongue of the wise brings healing.

Isaiah 58:8- Then your light will break forth like the dawn, and your healing will quickly appear; then your righteousness will go before you, and the glory of the Lord will be your rear guard.

Matthew 4:23-Jesus went throughout Galilee, teaching in their synagogues, proclaiming the good news of the kingdom, and healing every disease and sickness among the people.

Luke 6:19- and the people all tried to touch him, because power was coming from him and healing them all.

James 1:12- 12 Blessed is the one who perseveres under trial because, having stood the test, that person will receive the crown of life that the Lord has promised to those who love him.

From My Journey to Yours

Count it All Joy!

My heart was rejoicing as I thought about my pain
Said I'd count it all Joy if it's in Jesus's Name
So I set on my mission to evaluate my grief
Felt deeply depressed, could hardly eat or sleep
But I was nourished by the Word
 And resting in the arms of the Holy Spirit
Who enabled this broken heart to grin and bear it
I had a big plate of praise and large cup of grace
Supersized my prayer and added extra value to my closet space
Felt like I was imprisoned in my pain and being sentenced to life
Cuz a married man tricked me into believing he was divorced from his wife
Told lies so big…made Shaq look like a midget
And revenge is what I wanted even tho I couldn't get it
But I tried!
And God simply granted me access denied!
Cause the only thing that got hurt was my ego and my pride
Now I look back at those days and take it all in stride
Could've turned out worse, could've been crucified
Which is what our Savior endured…..
Took a beating of humiliation because He is our Lord
Became the sacrificial Lamb—and on the cross is where he died
And here I am crying over a little hurt pride
That's straight selfish, but the human side of me…
Just couldn't help it
Now I see that greater is He that is in me
Than he that is in the world
And the stench of idolatry mixed the funk of hatred
Are wiped out by the blood of Jesus and replaced with my Praises
Then my heart starts to rejoice when I think about that pain
Cuz I can count it all JOY when it's in Jesus's name!

James 1:2-5- ² Consider it pure joy, my brothers and sisters,[a] whenever you face trials of many kinds, ³ because you know that the testing of your faith produces perseverance. ⁴ Let perseverance finish its work so that you may be mature and complete, not lacking anything. ⁵ If any of you lacks wisdom, you should ask God, who gives generously to all without finding fault, and it will be given to you.

1 Chronicles 29:17- I know, my God, that you test the heart and are pleased with integrity. All these things I have given willingly and with honest intent. And now I have seen with joy how willingly your people who are here have given to you.

From My Journey to Yours

_____

_____

_____

_____

_____

_____

_____

_____

_____

_____

Eviction Notice

You've been living here rent free and haven't paid a dime
And I gave you the right to control all of my time
You eat what you want and don't buy any food
And I'm tip toeing around to see if you're in a good mood
You leave my house messy and start a bunch of confusion
And sit back entertained as if it's amusing
To watch me go through mess, while you're living a great life
While consummating our relationship, without me being your wife
When was it established that these were the rules?
You know that God protects little babies and fools?
Yes, I've been a fool to let you take charge of me
But now its time for you to go—You have to get out and away from me!!
You haven't paid a bill, It's only me who owes out money
 I even owe myself—and you might laugh, but that's not funny
Because I allowed you to occupy space and never pay rent
And now I'm in debt for all that I have spent
On your indulgence and influences because you knew how to get in
And tried to keep my account negative through all of my sin
That was fostered by your presence—the one that lived in me
Constantly hindering my ability to reach my true destiny
But its time for you to go—And this I will shout
"Here's your eviction notice—It's time for you to get out!!"
No you don't have thirty days— Immediately vacate my premises
You are a villain and a demon--an awful nemesis
You are not staying at this residence anymore
There's a whole big world out there for you to explore
I'm in enough debt and I don't need no more
Getting out of this debt, only God can restore
So get on out –it's time for you to go
No more entertainment and putting on a show
This vessel is God's and he occupies this home
He's the real King and He sits on the throne

Now, if you didn't hear me the first time-again I will shout "Here's your eviction notice—It's time for YOU to get OUT!!!"

Acts 19:12- so that even handkerchiefs and aprons that had touched him were taken to the sick, and their illnesses were cured and the evil spirits left them.

Matthew 8:31-The demons begged Jesus, "If you drive us out, send us into the herd of pigs."

Matthew 12:28-But if it is by the Spirit of God that I drive out demons, then the kingdom of God has come upon you.

From My Journey to Yours

_____

_____

_____

_____

_____

_____

_____

_____

_____

_____

_____

_____

His Will

The tighter I held on, the more you pulled away
But I only held on so tight because I really wanted you to stay
In my life as my protector, the one to keep me safe
From the bandits who robbed me and stripped me of my faith
But I'm sorry for expecting you to be more than you can
Especially at a time when you were in high demand
To life's problems that require a much higher force
To help a broken man get over his divorce
And to heal from the heartache from the investments he has made
In his family as he watches all of his dreams fade
Away into the darkness filled with anger and strife
Because the woman that betrayed his love called herself his wife
I wanted to be your friend because your heart seemed so sincere
But I liked the way it felt when you called me "baby" and "dear"
The feelings that overcame me were selfishly conceived
Because in my heart I wanted love and what you said is what I believed
I knew you couldn't love me before you healed from your own pain
And our relationship started in comfort, but ended in the shame
Of knowing what I saw in me was the fear I thought I'd left behind
To a past that keeps one tormented in spirit and in mind
So believe me when I tell you, I forgive your actions today
Because the heartache I was left with, forced me to kneel and pray
To the true and living God for my comfort and protection
Knowing full well about His death and resurrection
But still walking silently in the opposite direction
Of the path he created for each of us to travel
Smoothly through rough patches of rocks and gravel
Created from a foundation firmly set in stone
For me, a sinner, handed straight down from the throne
So my blessings from this tragedy is that I am able to heal
As long as I keep walking with God and do what's in His will.

1 Thessalonians 4:3-5-It is God's will that you should be sanctified: that you should avoid sexual immorality; that each of you should learn to control your own body in a way that is holy and honorable, not in passionate lust like the pagans, who do not know God;

1 Peter 2:15-For it is God's will that by doing good you should silence the ignorant talk of foolish people.

1 Peter 4:2- As a result, they do not live the rest of their earthly lives for evil human desires, but rather for the will of God.

From My Journey to Yours

Suds of Hope

I wash my soul with a special soap
One that lathers into Suds of Hope
Been thru ups and downs, suffered disappointments
But when washed clean with the Word of God, it's like a spiritual ointment
All my wounds are healed, my spirit restored,
And I, A filthy fragmented soul
Has been given another chance to be made whole
But fear sets in because of what may be in store
Will my secrets be revealed, show what I was before?
Like when I was used by the devil and made a spiritual wh^@#
Or will I be exposed as a surface believer?
The one that puts on a holy show instead of really telling
That life ain't been so blessed and its been smelling
As my lips get hot, like my mouth is set on fire
It keeps me reminded of the days from when I was liar
That's why I wash my soul with a special soap
One that lathers into Suds of Hope
My suds are a reminder of God's promises revealed
And the Hope comes from my wounds that have already been healed
Cuz each day I wake up I have chance to be cleansed
From the filth and debris and the blood on my hands
Been so excited about the Lord's divine plan for me
Bcuz hope for tomorrow sets my spirit free
Hope gives me Faith and my Faith gives me Hope
Keeping my special soap secure with my spiritual rope
And dropping it in the shower becomes a definite nope
Cuz the enemy waits for the prisoner in my mind
To be violently raped and robbed blind
So he can walk around and continue to boast
About how he has entered another Host
And stolen from God what he loves the most
Me! Or might say Us!
That's why I know, cleansing is a must

Romans 5: 3-5- 3 Not only so, but we[a] also glory in our sufferings, because we know that suffering produces perseverance; 4 perseverance, character; and character, hope. 5 And hope does not put us to shame, because God's love has been poured out into our hearts through the Holy Spirit, who has been given to us.

Job 13:15-Though he slay me, yet will I hope in him; I will surely defend my ways to his face.

2 Corinthians 1:20-For no matter how many promises God has made, they are "Yes" in Christ. And so through him the "Amen" is spoken by us to the glory of God.

From My Journey to Yours

_____

_____

_____

_____

_____

_____

_____

_____

_____

_____

The Battle is Won!!

My body is worn out –I'm being pulled in every direction
I want to crawl under a rock as my source of protection
But, I can't and I won't!!!!
And Even though I have free will, I've surrendered my choice
Because I'm submitted to Christ and I'm obedient to His voice
I won't walk in the flesh and fight against carnality
When it's a spiritual war that I'm fighting in actuality
I'm a humble servant of Christ and my soul is on fire
To walk in righteousness is a "Holy Spirit" desire
That boils in my heart and spews out of my soul
Leaving only the Lord over me— and He's rightfully in control
Of my life and direction in a world full of sin
People circling in the wilderness-it's repeating again!!
There's no weapons to use-Not a knife, sword, or gun
Let's fight because the battle has already been won
Our weapons of warfare are not of this world
Get up and fight for your soul
Don't walk in silence, it's time to scream and shout
"Devil you're time is up because Jesus just shut you out!"
Of the kingdom that's prepared for those who have overcome
By using the wisdom of the Lord and marching to the beat of His drum
How much more will it take before you see the Holy Ghost power?
Breakdown and destroy the unrighteous—we're at the zero hour!!
I'm tired and exhausted, my body is weak
But when I open my mouth, it's the Lord who speaks
Yes, His commandments live in the center of my heart
And He said from our lives He will never depart
So I take hold of His promises and its not always fun
But my joy is in knowing that the battle is already won!!!

2 Chronicles 20:17-You will not have to fight this battle. Take up your positions; stand firm and see the deliverance the Lord will give you,

Judah and Jerusalem. Do not be afraid; do not be discouraged. Go out to face them tomorrow, and the Lord will be with you.'"

Psalm 32:7-You are my hiding place; you will protect me from trouble and surround me with songs of deliverance.

Galatians 5:21-and envy; drunkenness, orgies, and the like. I warn you, as I did before, that those who live like this will not inherit the kingdom of God.

From My Journey to Yours

The Cure

I'm among the sick and I need a doctor
Been diagnosed with terminal Me, now I'm a walking X factor
My symptoms are doubt, worry, fear, and internal grief
Was bed ridden from lack of faith and paralysis gave me temporary relief
I took my fate as a joke—became a spiritual mocker
Placed my salvation in a box and lost the combination to the locker
Now I want to break free and God holds the only Key
To my cure
He unlocked my courage and "Boldness" broke open the door
Given me the opportunity to be once more restored
Cuz I willingly gave up my identity
Handing my soul to the World on a silver platter
While soul counts get higher and the World's belly gets fatter
Devouring the weak and preying on the strong
Selling death sentences and we buying them all
Leaving men, women, and children with broken spirits
That cry out so loud…only the heavens can hear it
And that works for me
Cuz I have to be directly connected sup-er-nat-urally
Forget the call center, don't put me on hold
It's time I pay the enemy back for his high interest loan
So I wrote a check in full and it was signed by Jesus Christ
Who paid for all of our freedom at a very high price
His Life!
So if you've been diagnosed with Terminal Me
Better get cured fast so you can live eternally!
Cuz dying is easy, but living is hard
Especially when stacked against you…are the enemy's odds.
So take the medicine of your redeemer and drink from the cup
What is pure
And you'll be forever healthy from the Jesus Christ cure.

Matthew 4:23- Jesus went throughout Galilee, teaching in their synagogues, proclaiming the good news of the kingdom, and healing every disease and sickness among the people.

Luke 5:17-One day Jesus was teaching, and Pharisees and teachers of the law were sitting there. They had come from every village of Galilee and from Judea and Jerusalem. And the power of the Lord was with Jesus to heal the sick.

Philippians 4:9-Whatever you have learned or received or heard from me, or seen in me—put it into practice. And the God of peace will be with you.

From My Journey to Yours

_____

_____

_____

_____

_____

_____

_____

_____

_____

_____

_____

_____

Bonus Poems

Free!

Wooly hair and cocoa brown skin, ivory teeth and a mustard seed of faith
That lives in my soul…
That's all I got!
Deep, deep down in my soul, I hear the voice of my Savior
The one who was born in the manger
Knows me better than me
Because I'm just a wandering stranger
Searching, searching for a resting place for my soul
Crying out everyday….Lord, please make me whole!
Seems I'm failing at life and becoming a worldly slave
Don't want to die without knowing the promise He gave.
Then I remember Galations 3:28
And my heart rejoices because it's not too late
I'm a child of God because of my faith in Christ
He gives me an identity as an heir to the promise
Of E-ternal life
I'm not just a color or label
But I am justified by faith
Given a chance to experience God's eternal grace!!!

Free! -- Part 2
Tucked away in the Motherland
And yes, God knows who I am.
Never Lost
Never forgotten
But given a word from Isaiah the prophet
Acts 8:25
One Ethiopian, guided and taught by the Lord's disciple
The love of God towards all humanity
Despite all the destruction and human calamity
We Are **One** in the body of Christ
All colors, all nations, all mankind
Are given an equal opportunity to walk with the divine

Don't miss your chance, cause I'm sure gone take mine
A song of praise wells up inside of me
A lily amongst thorns bestowed upon me
Not because I was born into slavery
But because it is Christ who died for us **ALL** to be free.

<u>Free – The end</u>
Now let's end with the beginning-A simple promise
Given in love with a magnificent blessing
Taught in the book of Genesis
From father Abram's obedience lesson
One Man
One God
One perfect choice
Written in biblical history as our ancestor's voice
A man whose heritage, color, and culture
Was invisibly molded into a spiritual sculpture
No physical attributes made him our father
It was faith and obedience
These remain the perfect ingredients
Of my wooly hair, and cocoa brown skin, ivory teeth
And a mustard seed of faith that lives in my soul
That's all I got!!!
That's all I need!!
Because I'd rather be a slave to Christ
If to the world, I'm made free!

Galations 3:28- [28] There is neither Jew nor Gentile, neither slave nor free, nor is there male and female, for you are all one in Christ Jesus.

Acts 8:25- [25] After they had further proclaimed the word of the Lord and testified about Jesus, Peter and John returned to Jerusalem, preaching the gospel in many Samaritan villages.

Ephesians 6:6-Obey them not only to win their favor when their eye is on you, but as slaves of Christ, doing the will of God from your heart.

From My Journey to Yours

The Prophetic Warrior

What's in a man who is obedient to God's voice?
He surrenders his own will and makes God's kingdom his first choice
No weapon formed against him shall prosper today
Because a man of God is stable and always finds his way
Into the presence of God, who has anointed his life
With wisdom, prosperity and an obedient wife
Greater is He that is in you than he that is in the world
Because the devil brings turmoil in a confusing swirl
Of physical attacks against a body, but that's only one's flesh
The brutal attack on the spirit is a warrior's true test
This case is not in court and you'll never need a lawyer
To tell you that God has sentenced you to be a prophetic warrior
The purpose that you serve and the blessings you are given
Are nothing short of the plan that God has purposely driven
In the lives of men who submit themselves to Christ
The devil won't ever fight fair--he's not in the business of being nice
It's known that the weapons of our warfare are mighty through God
And fighting to win is not complicated or hard
On the battlefield, the armor of God is worn
Without it, we're as naked and fragile as a newborn…
Fighting is exhausting--it makes a body tired and weak
But its God's strength that is heard when you open your mouth to speak
God occupies the space in the center of your heart
And with that said life will always live and death will always depart
So taking hold of His promises may not always be fun
But the joy is in knowing that the battle is already won!
Now, this case is closed and you don't need a courthouse a lawyer
To carry out your sentence of being God's Prophetic Warrior!!

Luke 11:49- Because of this, God in his wisdom said, 'I will send them prophets and apostles, some of whom they will kill and others they will persecute.'

2 Corinthians 9:13-Because of the service by which you have proved yourselves, others will praise God for the obedience that accompanies your confession of the gospel of Christ, and for your generosity in sharing with them and with everyone else.

From My Journey to Yours

_____

_____

_____

_____

_____

_____

_____

_____

_____

_____

_____

God's Grace

I'm confronting the closed doors that were shut in time and space
When my smile was stolen from my heart and my peace remained displaced
I became a child who never had a chance to grow
Into a woman with true love that I could proudly show
To my children and my parents and to those who mattered most
But during my journey of self-discovery my spirit was forced to grow
Into the woman that was lost inside me as a child
Who was so broken and so battered that I hardly ever smiled
At anyone because a Scarlett letter was imbedded on my chest
And I walked around in shame but always tried to do my best
To hide the deep dark secrets that blemished my soul
While broken into pieces with the desire to be whole
And for years I prayed for freedom and asked the Lord for His sweet grace
Of finally becoming the woman that had vanished without a trace
Of evidence because the thief left nothing behind to show
That he had violated me as a baby and stunted my spiritual growth
Into the woman who now stands right before your eyes
No longer hiding shame and wearing a disguise
By trying to be someone else and hiding from the blame
Of having to utter the words of my abductor's name
Because the Lord gave me back everything that was taken
He made His promises to me—And there is no mistaken
That what he said is what will be
He has come to set the captives free
And His promises are real because he didn't come to steal
My identity or my virtue, instead His awesome power healed
All the wounds inside that kept me away from His glory
So I can stand tall and tell my testimony or story
Of the blessings He has given and for those yet to come
Through the love he had bestowed upon His glorious kingdom
So I'm confronting the closed doors that were shut in time and space

And now I see God's blessing shining brightly on my face
And I humbly receive his mercy and his wonderful Sweet Grace.

Luke 12:8-"I tell you, whoever publicly acknowledges me before others, the Son of Man will also acknowledge before the angels of God.

2 Corinthians 9:14-And in their prayers for you their hearts will go out to you, because of the surpassing grace God has given you.

1 Peter 5:10-And the God of all grace, who called you to his eternal glory in Christ, after you have suffered a little while, will himself restore you and make you strong, firm and steadfast.

From My Journey to Yours

www.ingramcontent.com/pod-product-compliance
Lightning Source LLC
Chambersburg PA
CBHW072335300426
44109CB00042B/1630